ART AND WONDERS

JORDAN

Geographic & Co.

1
The Khasneh, Petra's most
famous building.

2-3
The brightly coloured desert
of Wadi Rum.

4 top
A Byzantine mosaic
found at Petra.

4-5
The Deir stands alone on a
hill that overlooks Petra.

TEXT
Fabio Bourbon

GRAPHIC DESIGN
Clara Zanotti

TRANSLATION
C. T. M., Milan

© 2000, 2008 White Star S.p.A.
Published by GEOGRAPHIC & CO
an imprint of: White Star S.p.A.
Via Candido Sassone, 22-24
13100 Vercelli, Italy

Distributed in Jordan by
REDWAN BOOK SHOP
Aqaba 77110 Jordan
Tel: + 962 (03) 201 3704
Fax : + 962 (03) 201 5588
redwanbook@hotmail.com

ISBN: 978-88-540-0201-2
2 3 4 5 6 12 11 10 09 08
Printed in Rotolito, Italy.

ART AND WONDERS

JORDAN

Contents

JORDAN IN FACTS AND FIGURES   PAGE   8

THE HISTORICAL PROGRESS OF THE COUNTRY   PAGE   10

AMMAN – A dynamic capital   PAGE   18

FOLKLORE AND CRAFTS –

The soul of the country   PAGE   34

ARAQ AL-AMIR – The fort of Hirkanus   PAGE   38

JERASH – The city of Artemis   PAGE   40

PELLA – Vicissitudes of history   PAGE   48

UMM QAYS - Ancient Gadara   PAGE   50

THE RIVER JORDAN –

The green heart of the country   PAGE   52

THE DEAD SEA – An oddity of nature   PAGE   56

MOUNT NEBO – The tomb of the Patriarch   PAGE   60

MADABA – The Holy Land revealed   PAGE   64

THE CASTLES OF THE DESERT –

Custodians of an epic past   PAGE   68

PETRA – The rose-red city of the Nabataeans   PAGE   80

WADI RUM – Lawrence's desert   PAGE 108

AQABA – The window on the Red Sea   PAGE 118

PHOTOGRAPHIC CREDITS   PAGE 128

5 top
A view of the elliptical forum
at Jerash.

5 bottom
A detail of a mosaic conserved
in the basilica on Mount Nebo.

5

Mediterranean
Sea

Israel

Egypt

✦ UMM QAYS
PELLA ✦   ✦ IRBID
          ✦ AJLUN
          ✦ JERASH
      ✦ SALT ✦ ZARQ
          ✦ AMMA
      ✦ MOUNT NEB
ZARQA MAIN ✦ ✦ MADABA

✦ KARAK

✦ ASH SHAWBAK

✦ PETRA
▲ JEBEL HARUN

✦ MA'AN

Wadi Rum

✦ AQABA ▲ JEBEL RUM

Jordan

Dead Sea

Gulf of Aqaba

JORDAN

Iraq

AFRAQ

✦ QASR EL AZRAQ
✦ AZRAQ
QASR EL KARANAH

Saudi
Arabia

7
*A typical village
near Amman.*

6 top
A beach at Aqaba.

6 bottom
*The red rock formations at
Wadi Rum.*

Jordan in facts and figures
A GEOGRAPHICAL OUTLINE OF THE COUNTRY

8

Jordan seen from space.

8-9

This satellite picture clearly shows the Gulf of Aqaba, Wadi Arabah, the Dead Sea and the river Jordan.

9 bottom

A satellite view of the desert in eastern Jordan.

Jordan covers 37,737 square miles and is bordered to the north by Syria, to the north-east by Iraq, to the south and south-west by Saudi Arabia and to the west by Israel and the Palestine National Authority. The country is divided into two distinct geographical regions: to the east is the vast desert tableland of Transjordan and to the west is Ghor, the deep tectonic depression that stretches from the western borders to the Gulf of Aqaba, taking in the Jordan valley, the Dead Sea and Wadi Arabah. The immense fault-line known as the Great Rift Valley was formed between 40 and 25 million years ago bounded to the east by the heights of the tableland. These elevations are profoundly marked by valleys created by seasonal water courses that give life to a landscape that is as extreme as it is beautiful. The expanses of desert to the east are interrupted by isolated rock massifs, the highest of which are Jebel ar-Rimah (4,016 feet) and Jebel al-Asfar (3,521 feet). The highlands north of Amman are dominated by the Ajlun massif (4,091 feet) but the tallest peaks in Jordan are Jebel Mubarak (5,665 feet) and Jebel Rum (5,755 feet) along the Ghor depression in the south of the country.

Jordan's climate is hot and dry with little rainfall, even more so in the south and east. Much of the country is therefore arid with

the only fertile areas being the valleys of the river Jordan and its few tributaries where Mediterranean *maquis* prevails. Isolated oases are found in the eastern desert, the largest of which is Azraq.

As there is an insufficient capacity of river water, the government has invested large sums in the construction of water storage basins which are used for irrigation and the production of electricity. These have encouraged agriculture, the produce of which is important in a country that is otherwise poor in natural resources (only phosphates and potash are found in abundance); stock raising, like industrialisation, is in slow but constant growth.

10 top
A map of Wadi Sabra
near Petra.

10-11
The fort in Aqaba.

PLAN
de
OUADI·SABRA.

The historical progress of the country

10 bottom left

Jebel Harun, also known as Mount Hor.

10 bottom right

The Gulf of Aqaba.

11

…éon de Laborde in Bedouin tume (the lithographs on these …ges are taken from the book, …oyage de l'Arabie Pétrée, Léon de Laborde, 1830).

During the Palaeolithic era, the region known today as Jordan was inhabited by groups of hunter-gatherers constantly on the move in search of edible plants and game. Many semi-permanent settlements have been discovered in the Jordan valley near Azraq.

From about 9000 BC, i.e. during the Neolithic or Natufian epoch, small communities dedicated to agriculture and the raising of domestic animals were formed. One of the settlements that can be dated to this era has been found at el-Beidha, a little north of Petra. A little later, the villages in the southernmost areas were abandoned, perhaps due to a worsening of the climate; on the other hand, camps of nomadic peoples, whose presence until the seventh century BC can be proven, survived. Villages in the Jordan valley and other northern hill areas continued to prosper: at one of the oldest known "cities" – Ain Ghazal near Amman – murals and near life-size statues have been found. The first copper articles appeared towards the Calcolithic era (4500 BC – 3000 BC). During the Bronze Age at the end of the fourth millennium BC, various urban centres surrounded by defensive walls were built. At the start of the third millennium BC, the first written documents began to appear in the form of tablets bearing cuneiform characters. The Semitic Amorite people settled along the river Jordan from about 2200 BC while culture felt the twin influences of Syria and Egypt. The following six centuries saw invasion by the vaguely identified Sea-Peoples and the expansion campaigns of the Egyptian pharaohs that were withstood by the Hittite princes. In an era that has been fixed as being around 1500 BC, the Bible claims that a people called the Orites settled in the valley of Petra; they were then chased out by the Semitic Edomite tribe which came to occupy the region between the Gulf of Aqaba and the Dead Sea around the thirteenth century BC. During the same period, the kingdoms of Moab and Ammon prospered, the latter having *Rabbath Ammon*

(present-day Amman) as capital.

The Edomites claimed to be descended directly from Esau and therefore belonged to the dynastic line of Moses but it is certain that their relations with the Israelites were extremely poor for several centuries; after the fall of Jerusalem to the Babylonians in 587 BC, the inhabitants of Edom attacked and plundered the kingdom of Judaea on several occasions. The Edomites, however, were being put under increasing pressure by a nomadic people, the Nabataeans, who spoke a derivation of Aramaic and came from the Arabian peninsula. In the end, the Edomites were completely supplanted by the new tribe. The Nabataeans are cited with certainty for the first time in a fourth-century-BC document but it is evident that their infiltration had begun much earlier. A hard, determined and ingenious people that lived by grazing, they

survived in the desert by digging water cisterns out of the rock in which the rare rainwater would be conserved during the dry months. Their prosperity was the result of their control of caravan routes between Arabia and the Mediterranean and between Egypt and Mesopotamia, a control they maintained ever after they had settled at Petra. From the fourth century BC the Nabataeans resisted attempts to subject them by the successors of Alexander the Great (first Antigonus Monofthalmus, then the Ptolemies of Egypt and finally the Seleucids of Syria). During their period of maximum glory, between the first century BC and the first century AD, the Nabataean kingdom stretched from Hegra in the Arabian desert to the cities of the Negev (Advat, Mamshit and Shivta in Israel) and Damascus. From 64 BC, the armies of Rome began their conquest of Palestine and Syria; the hellenised cities east of the river Jordan (Amman, Jerash, Pella, Gadara and others) fell to the Romans and were associated in the league known as the *Decapolis*. The Nabataean kingdom formally remained independent until 106 when Emperor Trajan annexed it to the province of Arabia. At least two centuries of well-being followed, thanks to the road that Trajan had

built from Aqaba to Damascus to encourage commercial traffic.

When the Roman empire was divided into two, the territories to the east of the Jordan — where Christianity had spread since the third century — fell under the influence of Byzantium. During the sixth century control of these lands was entrusted to the Ghassanids, Christian Arabs in permanent struggle against the Sassanians. In 628, the Arabs led by Mohammed defeated the Byzantines near Karak. This victory marked the start of the Islamisation of the region that was dominated

by the Umayyad dynasty from 661 to 750. The Umayyads were replaced by the Abbasid caliphs, and then by the Fatimids who were in turn substituted by the Turkish Seljuks in 1071. In the meantime, the local economy had been increasingly impoverished and the bloody era of the Crusades (eleventh and twelfth century) did not improve the situation. The Crusaders created the Latin kingdom of Jerusalem and built a series of castles in Transjordan (including those of Karak and Shawbak) but were defeated in 1187 by the sultan Salah al-Din, better known as Saladin.

12 left
The Roman theatre in Wadi Sabra near Petra.

12 top right
The pronaos in the Khasneh at Petra.

12-13
The depression of Wadi Arabah and Jebel Harun.

12 bottom right
The tomb of Uneishu at Petra.

In 1260 Palestine and Transjordan were subjected by the Mamelukes, warrior sultans that reigned until 1516 when they were chased out by the Turkish Ottomans whose domination lasted over 400 years.

Their rule was, however, a period of substantial stagnation broken between 1870 and 1890 by the immigration of Circassian communities that repopulated many cities that had been abandoned for centuries: Amman, Jerash and many others. Following the defeat of the Crusaders, Transjordan had become a

little known land in the West and even the magnificent city of Petra had been forgotten. This situation lasted until the start of the nineteenth century when several European travellers began to explore these fabulous lands. Petra was rediscovered in 1812 by Johann Ludwig Burckhardt, a young Swiss explorer and orientalist who spoke Arabic fluently and who travelled under false pretences as a sheikh. The first reliable pictures of the rock city were the work of the French count, Léon de Laborde and his travelling companion, Louis Linant de Bellefonds, who arrived in Petra in 1828. Once they returned to France in 1830, Laborde published his account of the expedition

14 top
The Gate of Temenos
at Petra.

14 bottom
The pronaos of the Khasneh
at Petra.

15
The Khasneh at Petra (the
lithographs on these pages
are taken from "The
Holy Land", by David
Roberts, 1842-1846).

accompanied by dozens of lithographs. The volume, *"Voyage de l'Arabie Pétrée"*, signalled the start of scientific knowledge of the Levant and the Nabataean capital. In March 1839, the Scot, David Roberts — one of the best known landscape artists of his time — visited Petra. Although he made no more than 14, his views of the "rose-red city" are among the loveliest the artist ever produced.

Following this first period of fame in the West, Transjordan returned to the fore during World War I. This was when the rebellion of the local sheikhs broke out against the Turkish

sultan who was now considered a foreign oppressor. The Hashemite emir, Hussein Ibn Ali (1853-1931), started the rebellion and in 1916 entrusted his sons, Abdullah and Feisal, with command of guerrilla operations strategically assisted by the British. This was the period during which the legend of Lawrence of Arabia (Thomas Edward Lawrence, 1888-1935) was born; he was the British officer that led the victorious attack against the Turkish fort in Aqaba. Following the definitive defeat of the Ottomans (October 1918), the Emirate of Transjordan became a League of Nations mandate under Great Britain in 1921 with Abdullah as emir. In 1946, the country finally became independent and the emir took the title of king. After occupation of Cisjordan in 1950, the country was renamed Jordan. Following the assassination of King Abdullah and the short-lived accession of his son Talal, Hussein II mounted the throne in July 1953 and reigned over the country until 1999. This was a difficult period marked by two wars against Israel, mass immigration of Palestinian refugees, repression of PLO terrorism and by the crisis of the Gulf War.

Today the Hashemite kingdom of Jordan is a constitutional hereditary monarchy. The king is the head of state and leader of the executive and appoints the Council of Ministers. Legislative power is the responsibility of the National Assembly which is formed by the Chamber of Deputies and the Senate.

The population of Jordan is roughly 4.3 million, the great majority being Sunni Moslems (Christians number less than 4%). Due to the aridity of most of the country, the most densely occupied areas are the Jordan valley and the mountains north of Amman which receive much higher rainfall than the rest of the country. Almost 80% of Jordanians live in the capital and the main urban centres: Zarqa (practically a suburb of Amman), Irbid, Mafraq, Balqa, Karak, Tafila and Ma'an. The ethnic composition is rather complex: in general, it can be said that half the population is descended from tribes of Arab origin that have been settled in Jordan since immemorial time. Palestinians more or less make up the

15 bottom right
This famous portrait
of David Roberts in oriental

dress was painted in
1840 by Robert Scott
Launder.

15

16 top
Petra: the Siq gorge and the triumphal arch that collapsed in 1896.

16 bottom
The Palace Tomb and the Corinthian Tomb at Petra.

16-17
The Deir, one of the best preserved monuments at Petra.

17 top
Petra, a group of Bedouins.

17 bottom
Nabataean tombs in the outer Siq at Petra (the lithographs on these pages are taken from "The Holy Land", by David Roberts, 1842-1846).

other half who have arrived in waves since 1948 when the state of Israel was founded, then again following Jewish occupation of Cisjordan and, finally, during the war in Kuwait. They have been widely assimilated into society and many occupy important positions in political and economic fields. Then there are the Bedouin, mostly permanently settled now, with only 40,000 still nomadic. They are proud, reserved and educated in a sort of chivalric code. They are also very much respected, perhaps because they played a crucial role in the war of independence against the Ottomans. The army's most respected troop and the Royal Guard are mostly Bedouin. Besides the several Christian minorities, mostly Greek Orthodox and Greek Catholics, Jordan's ethnic

tourists who are mostly attracted by the ancient cities of Petra and Gerasa. There have also been rapid changes from a social and cultural point of view: the number of schools has increased dramatically and now Jordan is the Arab country with the highest rate of literacy.

For the tourist, Jordan is without doubt one of the safest and most enjoyable countries to visit. It has many examples of natural and artistic beauty and is full of pleasurable surprises.

The following pages are a succinct but, we believe, exhaustive introduction to this extraordinary country. Welcome to Jordan!

picture is completed by Circassians, Islamised Caucasians that arrived in Jordan in the nineteenth century. It was they who reintroduced agriculture to the country, an activity that had been abandoned at the end of the Umayyad era.

Modern Jordan is a country undergoing rapid development and looking to the future. Under the enlightened guidance of the lamented King Hussein II (who was succeeded in 1999 by his son Abdullah), the Jordanian economy has succeeded in coping with many crises. In just a few years, the network of roads has been greatly increased, dams and electric power stations have been built, and the sea port at Aqaba has been expanded and modernised. Peace with Israel, signed in 1994, has brought a substantial increase in international

Amman

A DYNAMIC CAPITAL

18
The city of Amman is largely modern and stretches over nineteen hills (or jebel).

18-19
In just three decades, Amman's physical size has doubled.

19
Despite the traffic, the Jordanian capital is still a liveable city.

A Middle Eastern city *par excellence*, the minarets of its mosques piercing the extraordinary blue of the Jordanian sky, the narrow alleys of the centre crowded with whitewashed houses, the coloured crowd in incessant movement, Amman welcomes its visitors with a warm and relaxing atmosphere, clean streets, friendly inhabitants and freshly restored monuments. Despite growing at a dizzying rate (in 1970 it had 570 thousand residents, at the end of the 1990's almost 2 million), Amman is one of the most ordered Arab capitals and unquestionably one of the most liveable. It is a modern and dynamic metropolis in which the traffic moves more smoothly than in many large European cities thanks to the use of roundabouts and wide avenues that wind around the bases of the low hills on which the residential area has been built. Like Rome, Amman was founded on seven hills (*jebel*) but now covers nineteen. Seat of government, the parliament and the official residence of the king, Amman has recently made itself into an important business centre as a meeting place for the economies and societies of the Arab and western worlds. Its huge commercial expansion has developed at an equal pace with its urban growth so that the lower city – or historic centre – is now encircled by large residential districts and an

efficient road network that gives easy communications with the rest of the country. Since the industrial districts are concentrated in outlying areas, Amman is not very polluted, a truly valuable boon in the modern world. The large futuristic buildings, university, banks, embassies, offices of foreign multinational companies, luxury hotels, shops and fashionable meeting places are only one aspect of this fascinating and atmospheric city that has managed to conserve the traces of its 3000-year-old history among so many signs of modern civilisation.

From up on the Citadel one can see the vestiges of an important past and the dozens of minarets attesting Amman's devotion to the teachings of Islam. In the centre of the city stands the Mosque of Hussein, rebuilt in 1924 and named after the emir that brought life to modern-day Jordan.

21 centre
The Mosque of Malik
Abdullah was completed in
1990.

21 bottom
Friday prayers in the
square in front of the
Mosque of Hussein.

20-21
The mosque of Abu Darvish
is unusual for its two-
coloured surface.

21 top
Founded in the seventh
century, the Mosque of
Hussein was rebuilt in 1924
and completed in 1987.

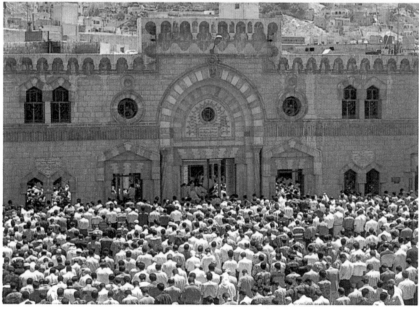

The contrast of black and white construction materials in the characteristic Mosque of Abu Darvish stand out on the peak of Jebel Ashrafiyah. The Mosque of Malik Abdullah, on the other hand, is unmistakable with its large dome lined with light blue majolica and two slender minarets; completed in 1990, it has already become the symbol of the Amman that looks to the future. The unusual contrast between ancient and modern buildings without an intermediary section is one of the most apparent characteristics of the Jordanian capital.

This is because, after the splendours of the past, Amman fell into decline and was completely abandoned from the thirteenth century to 1920 when it was re-founded as the result of a political decision taken after the fall of the Ottoman empire. The same contrast is seen as one passes from the large traffic avenues into the labyrinthine alleys of the lower city between Jebel at-Taj and Jebel al-Qalah, or by threading one's way between the coloured stalls in the *souk* near the Mosque of Hussein. Along with the smell of coffee

22 top
The souk in Amman sells everything from spices to cotton T-shirts.

22 bottom
The souk is an excellent place for doing business; it is situated near the Mosque of Hussein.

22-23
Other typical places for business and social meetings are the cafés where the narghilé is always present.

23 bottom
Many farmers come to the city to sell their products in the souk.

24-25
The Mosque of Hussein at dusk.

24 bottom left
A view of the Mosque of Abu Darvish by night.

24 bottom right
Evening shadows fall over one of the central streets.

and the pungent perfume of spices, here one breathes the true atmosphere of the Middle East. The vegetable sellers and fruiterers vie for space with sellers of clothes and fabrics, coppersmiths offer embossed bowls, plates and pots and, further down, a seller declaims the quality of his carpets. Shopkeepers, craftsmen and pedlars carrying cool drinks or baskets filled with the most disparate goods keep alive a tradition that seems eternal. With its bright colours and knots of shoppers who stop to examine goods and enter lengthy negotiations over prices, the market in Amman offers an unforgettable cross-section of daily life. The bustle of the *souk*, and indeed of all hardworking Amman, only quietens after dusk when the city wraps itself in the magic of the night below a star-studded sky that seems vaster here than elsewhere. The hills are covered with a myriad of glimmering lights and, higher, the luminous bunting of the minarets.

It is impossible to remain unmoved by Amman and it was not by chance that the

25 top
An illuminated fountain in a central square.

25 centre
The Roman theatre seen from the Citadel at dusk.

25 bottom
Another view of the centre from the Citadel.

Romans, who were experts in city planning, built here some of the most spectacular constructions in the eastern provinces of the empire. At the time, Amman went by the name of *Philadelphia*; it was part of the *Decapolis* and very wealthy thanks to its strategic position on the caravan route from Bosra in Syria to Petra and the Gulf of Aqaba. Even today, great imperial ruins stand among the modern buildings; for example, the 6000-seat Theatre that is still in use, next to it is the Odeon, the Forum and, on the hill of the Citadel, the temple dedicated to Hercules.

The origins of Amman are not Roman, however, as the city existed in biblical times when it was the capital of the Ammonites with the name of *Rabbath Ammon*. It later became Israelite, then Ammonite once more, later Assyrian and Babylonian before falling into the hands of the Ptolemies of Egypt; later again it was taken by the Seleucids of Syria and then the Nabataeans. Conquered by Rome in 30 BC, it experienced its maximum splendour in the second and third centuries before becoming a Byzantine city, and then being taken by the Arabs in 635. It went into slow decline before its abandonment and remained uninhabited until 1868 when it was repopulated. Elected capital of Transjordan in 1921 and of Jordan in 1950, today Amman is a young city just 3000 years old.

28-29 and 29 top
The ruins of the Temple of Hercules stand on the hill of the Citadel. It was built in honour of Emperor Marcus Aurelius around 170 AD.

29 centre and 29 bottom
The oldest section of Amman stands on the hill of the Citadel; the remains of the Qasr, a palace from the Umayyad era (720-750 AD) can be seen here today.

30 top left
This female head found in Amman has been dated to the second century AD.

30-31 and 30 bottom left
The National Archaeological Museum inside the Citadel has a collection of finds from all over Jordan.

30 bottom right
These famous seventh century, two-faced heads perhaps served as capitals.

31 bottom left
This second century head of Tyche was found in the courtyard of the Museum.

31 bottom right
This splendid stone panel decorated the Gate of Temenos in Petra.

32 top
*Palestinian clothes in the
Museum of Popular Traditions.*

32 centre
Traditional Bedouin clothes.

32 bottom
This is a reconstruction of a
Bedouin caravan in a room
in the Folklore Museum.

32-33
The Museum of Popular
Traditions is housed in part
of the Roman Theatre.

33 bottom left
Women's clothing typical of
Karak displayed in the
Museum of Folklore.

33 bottom right
The interior of a typical Jordanian
house has been reconstructed in the
Folklore Museum.

Folklore and crafts
THE SOUL OF THE COUNTRY

On a broad basis, Jordan shares its folklore with that of other Middle Eastern countries though it has its local peculiarities. For example, it seems that Jordanians prefer to drink coffee to the traditional mint tea; they like it ground very fine and boiled directly in the water together with sugar and perfumed with cardamom. It is common to come across pedlars selling this sweet-smelling drink in any town or village and should be tried at least once. Equally common are the sellers of *chai* (mint tea) which is a real pick-me-up at the hottest time of the day. Jordanian cooking is very seasoned and typical dishes, often presented very attractively, are excellent: well worth trying are *kibbeh* (lamb meat balls with spices and sesame seeds), *musakhan* (steamed chicken served with a tasty sauce), *shish kebab* (lamb on skewers), *maqluba* (chicken or beef stew with vegetables) and *falafel* (balls of chick pea flour mixed with spices) but there are many more. In any case, *khobz taabun*, the round Arab bread, is delicious.

34 top
A seller of semi-precious stones in the souk in Amman.

34 centre
Spices are cheap and of excellent quality.

34 bottom
A typical tea seller near Amman.

34-35
Another tea seller, this time in the market in Irbid.

35 bottom left
A food shop in one of the multicoloured streets of Irbid.

35 bottom right
A woman preparing the typical Arab bread.

Local crafts also have much to offer. Jordanian taste in art is mostly expressed in the production of glass items, pottery, jewellery, inlaid wood, embroidery and the well-known small bottles of coloured sand. The arrangements of coloured grains reaches levels of perfection and creates work for many youngsters. The art of the mosaic is very old and is particularly noted at Madaba where there is a professional school that turns out craftsmen of the highest levels. Carpet weaving is another typical activity which is now mostly performed in modern workshops but in accordance with the ancient methods. The masters of this trade are the Bedouin who live around Madaba, Karak, Tafilah and in Wadi Rum. As far as tourists are concerned, there is a surfeit of choice.

36 top
Bottles of coloured sand are one of the country's most popular souvenirs.

36 centre
The most important virtue for this young worker is patience.

36 bottom
A young girl at work in the mosaic school in Madaba.

36-37
*A woman weaving
a carpet using traditional
methods.*

37 bottom left
*Modern glasswork takes
its inspiration from
the past.*

37 bottom right
*The value of a carpet
depends on the density of
knots which create it.*

38-39
The Qasr al-Abd is one of the few Hellenistic civil buildings to have survived to the present.

38 bottom left
The remains of the defensive walls around Qasr al-Abd date from the Byzantine era.

38 bottom right
Wadi as-Sir is a picturesque village near Araq al-Amir.

39 top
Male and female lions decorate the frieze that runs along the upper floor of the palace.

Araq al-Amir
THE FORT OF HIRKANUS

The itinerary that follows aims to indicate the most important and interesting historical and archaeological sites as well as the loveliest areas of the countryside. The route starts from Amman from which all distances are calculated.

The locality Araq al-Amir is situated about 14 miles from the capital and is known for the ruins of a "fort" that was constructed during the third century BC. It is prettily located in the middle of a natural amphitheatre which may originally have been the centre of a small artificial lake. The fort is rectangular with a massive tower at each corner of which only their lower sections remain. The building was built using enormous blocks of stone, some of which weigh 20 tonnes. It seems certain that it had two floors with large tanks used to collect water. Stores for foodstuffs were on the ground floor while the upper storey was used for habitation. A porch with two columns on the northern side is topped by a frieze depicting lions and lionesses that continues on the outer sides of the angular towers. Above the frieze, a loggia was built with six columns which correspond to the wide windows in the towers, each divided by two columns. The long sides of the structure each have seven windows while the south face also has a porch similar to the one on the north side but destroyed above the trabeation. Rather than a fort, it seems that Qasr al-Abd was actually a residential palace built by Hirkanus, a member of the powerful Tobiad family that created a small "buffer" kingdom in the region contested between the Ptolemies of Egypt and the Seleucids of Syria.

40 top
View of the Cardo
Maximus.

40 bottom
The north tetrapylon *at the
crossing of the Cardo with
the northern Decuman.*

41 bottom right
*The triumphal arch named
after Emperor Hadrian.*

Jerash
THE CITY OF ARTEMIS

The ancient city of Gerasa, known by the modern name of Jerash, lies in a wide valley about 30 miles from Amman. It was founded in the fourth century BC by Semitic peoples on a site that had been occupied during Neolithic times. During its Greek colonisation, Gerasa flourished as a trading centre and when it entered the Roman sphere of influence during the last decades of the first century BC, it was one of

Legend

1	TRIUMPHAL ARCH	11	SOUTH TETRAPYLON	18 CHURCH OF ST. JOHN
2	HIPPODROME	12	CATHEDRAL	19 CHURCH OF ST. GEORGE
3	REST HOUSE	13	NYMPHAEUM	20 CHURCH OF SS. PETER AND PAUL
4	SOUTH GATE	14	CHURCH OF THE PROPYLAEA	21 NORTH THEATRE
5	TEMPLE OF ZEUS	15	TEMPLE OF ARTEMIS	22 THERMAE
6	FORUM	16	CHURCH OF ST. THEODORE	23 NORTH TETRAPYLON
7	SOUTH THEATRE	17	CHURCH OF SS.	
8	CARDO MAXIMUS			
9	MUSEUM			

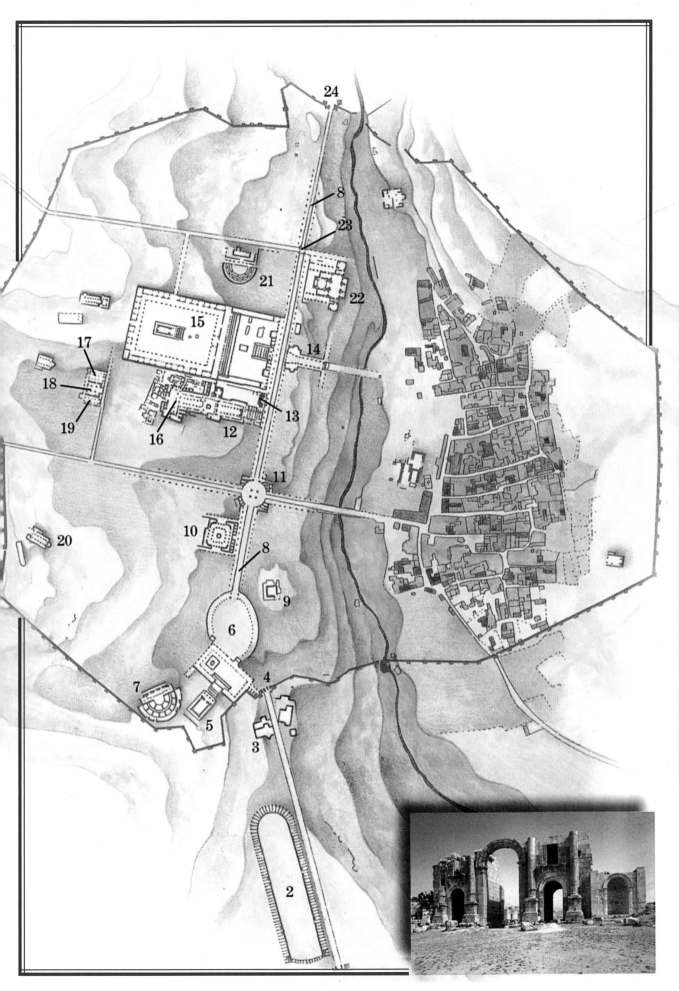

the main cities in the *Decapolis*, a confederation of ten cities of which Gerasa is today the best conserved. From the second half of the first century AD, it enjoyed great prosperity from trade with caravans and it reached the apex of its wealth during the age of Anthony. After a period of decline in the third and fourth centuries, Gerasa (which had become Christian) enjoyed another period of affluence under Emperor Justinian (527-566) when a number of churches with mosaic floors were built. The city was razed to the ground during the Crusades and finally abandoned to be repopulated from 1878 but the excellent state of conservation of the city's Roman and Byzantine buildings is the direct result of its long centuries of oblivion.

The plan of the ancient city – whose eastern sector is now mostly occupied by modern buildings – is characterised by the city's long principal road that runs north-south (the *Cardo Maximus*) intersected at right angles by two other roads (the *Decuman*) which cross the river in the central area over bridges. A majestic, 3-vault triumphal arch stands outside the southern

43 bottom
*The south theatre built
during the first century AD
during Domitian's reign.*

44-45
*The south face of the Temple
of Artemis and some of the
columns in the holy area.*

44 bottom left
*An unusual view of the
columns in the Temple of
Artemis.*

gate that was built in 130 AD to celebrate the visit of Emperor Hadrian. A hippodrome was built next to it during the mid-second century AD measuring 265 yards long and capable of seating 15,000 people. The Jerash Rest House stands near the southern gate which also acts as an information centre and restaurant.

Entering the city, the visitor comes to the temple of Zeus built in 163 AD with eight columns on the frontage, and the south theatre which could hold 3000 spectators. The unusual *Forum*, measuring 98 yards along its main axis, stands right in front of the temple of Zeus and is a unique example of its kind. Rather than the usual rectangular design, it is elliptical and surrounded by a portico of Ionic columns that covered a row of shops. For this reason, it has been thought that the *Forum* in Gerasa predominantly existed for economic rather than political and religious reasons, an argument that is supported by the fact that it lies away from the centre of the city. If that is true, the Romans would have let the large temple of Artemis in the centre of the city act as Gerasa's social and spiritual life.

46 top
The Ionic capital on one of the columns in the Forum.

46 centre
The Forum and, right, a view of the Temple of Zeus.

46 bottom
A detail from the Temple of Zeus built in 163 AD; the columns are 46 feet high.

46-47
The unusually shaped elliptical Forum in Gerasa that measures 98 yards by 87.

The hexastyle, peripteral temple dedicated to the patron goddess of Gerasa stands in the centre of a nine-acre holy area which was reached from the *Cardo* via a magnificent flight of steps. Nearby stood a large nymphaeum with an exedra occupied by an ornamental bath.

Among the other Roman monuments, there is a second theatre in the northern section of the city, two Roman baths – one on each side of the river – a large four-faced arch in the centre of a circular square along the *Cardo* and a similar but less grand *tetrapylon* on the same road which continued out of the north gate. The *Cardo* was flanked for a fair distance by a series of tombs as far as a small theatre built during Anthony's reign near a large tank that may have been used for aquatic displays.

Of special interest are the Archaeological Museum not far to the east of the forum and the Christian churches (in particular those of SS. Peter and Paul, the *Propylaea*, St. Theodore and SS. Cosma and Damian).

48 top
One of the Corinthian
capitals in the Byzantine
basilica.

Pella

THE VICISSITUDES OF HISTORY

Pella shares its name with the ancient capital of Macedonia. Built less than 60 miles north of Amman, the ruins of the ancient town centre (excavated since 1979) stand near the modest village of Tabaqat al-Fahl whose livelihood depends on it. Founded by some officers from Alexander the Great's army around 310 BC on a site that had been inhabited in the Neolithic era and with a good supply of fresh water, the town grew prosperous from trade and its advantageous position in the Jordan valley. Under Roman occupation it was a member of the *Decapolis* and in 70 AD offered refuge to Christians fleeing from Jerusalem under siege from Emperor Titus. The city's peak of grandeur was reached in the first and second centuries; the remains of a small theatre built during that period have been unearthed near the edge of the steep valley of Wadi Jirm al Moz.

Up to the third century, Pella went into a slow decline which was only halted during the Byzantine epoch (between the fifth and the sixth century) when at least three churches and a large, three-nave basilica with Corinthian columns were built.

In 635, Moslem armies defeated the Christians near the city and Pella was given the name of *Fahl*. During the Umayyad dynasty, there was ceaseless construction including the building of an impressive mosque. In 746, a violent earthquake completely destroyed the centre and the town remained uninhabited until the tenth century when it was occupied by the Abbasids. During Mameluke domination, a mosque was built (fifteenth-sixteenth century) which is still in use today. Besides the remains of the theatre and the Christian basilica, the ruins of the temple of Zeus Areios can be admired.

48 bottom
The large, three-nave basilica was built when Pella was a bishopric.

48-49
During the Roman era, Pella was as large as Gerasa.

49 bottom left
Another view of the basilica with the columns raised during excavations.

49 bottom right
A large flight of steps led to the Byzantine basilica.

50-51
The west theatre made from black basalt.

50 bottom left
A basalt sarcophagus displayed in the local museum.

50 bottom right
The Archaeological Museum in the Ottoman village.

Umm Qays
ANCIENT GADARA

51 top
Several outstanding Roman statues are on display in the Archaeological Museum.

51 bottom
The Corinthian columns of the basilica and, in the background, the columns of the four-sided portico.

Umm Qays, ancient Gadara, was founded in the fourth century BC by veterans of Alexander the Great's army and during the Roman era was a member state of the *Decapolis*. In antiquity it was famous for being the birth-place of the philophers Menippus and Philodemus and the poet Meleager. Situated nearly 16 miles from Irbid and 55 miles from Amman, remains of its glorious past as a rich trading and caravan town are still visible. Many of its archaeological ruins date from the first half of the second century AD, its period of maximum economic and architectural splendour. An episcopal seat during the fourth century, Gadara was destroyed by an earthquake in 746.

Its most interesting buildings are the tombs in the eastern necropolis (with the sepulchres of the Germans, Modestus and Kaireas), the northern and western theatres, a colonnaded street, the baths, a four-sided portico, a basilica, the *nymphaeum*, the west gate next to a superb underground vault from the Roman period, the monumental gate and the hippodrome.

The river Jordan
THE GREEN HEART OF THE COUNTRY

The source of the river Jordan lies on the slopes of Mount Hermon the snows of which contribute to the water from the various springs found across the Golan heights. After flowing into Lake Tiberias, the Jordan winds its way to the Dead Sea along a fertile valley at an altitude entirely below the level of the not too distant Mediterranean. For 69 of its total 225 miles, the river's course marks the border between the state of Israel and the Palestine National Authority.

As the Jordan valley enjoys a mild climate in winter, the vegetation is luxuriant and varied. Pistachios, bananas, water-melons and grapefruit grow without difficulty. Jordanian agriculture has made notable progress in this region over the last few years: hothouses, fields and fruit and vegetable orchards irrigated by the river via a complex system of channels, piping, dams and artificial basins supply local markets with high quality produce. Thanks to the agricultural estates managed using modern methods, Jordan is able to export vegetables and fruit. The most important horticultural produce from an economic point of view are tomatoes, potatoes and lentils while the most common fruit are mandarins, lemons, apples and bananas. In particular, the plantations that cover a quarter of

52 centre
The apple orchards are still maintained manually.

52 bottom
Trees in blossom and fields in the fertile Jordan valley.

52-53
Water is a precious source of life.

53 bottom left
A crop of aubergines.

53 bottom right
There are many vineyards in the Jordan valley.

cultivatable land produce far more tomatoes than the national requirement and the sale of the surplus brings precious foreign currency. The same is true of olives, oil and figs. Almost 12,350 acres of land are planted with vines which produce white grapes of excellent quality, some of which are eaten and the rest of which go to the wine-making industry. Faced with such fertility, it is not difficult to imagine that the biblical description of the Garden of Eden was suggested by the green valley of the river Jordan.

54 top
Another view of the fertile Jordan valley.

54 bottom
Water is an important resource in an arid country like Jordan; this is also true for Wadi Zarqa, a small tributary of the Dead Sea.

54-55
The splendid waterfall of Wadi Zarqa is fed by hot springs rich in minerals.

55 bottom left
Another view of the waterfall in Wadi Zarqa.

55 bottom right
Olive groves in the Jordan valley.

56 top
*Mud taken from the shores
of the Dead Sea has many
therapeutic qualities.*

56 bottom
*Bathers in the Dead Sea
float as though lying on a
deckchair due to the
density of the water.*

The Dead Sea
AN ODDITY OF NATURE

The Dead Sea, 48 miles long by 10 at its widest point, lies in the deepest tectonic trench on the earth's surface, a full 1294 feet below the level of the Mediterranean. This surreal body of water is surrounded by an arid landscape on both the Jordanian and Israeli shores and it is only in the northern area near the inlet of the river Jordan that the moisture allows a little vegetation to exist. The sea, seven times saltier than any other on the planet and so dense that it is impossible to sink in it, was formed about a million years ago when the African continent separated from the plate that included Turkey and the Middle East. It is fed only by the river Jordan and a few *wadi* on the eastern side and it has no outlet. Its waters are completely devoid of life and have such a high content of magnesium, sodium, calcium, bromide and potassium that bathers have to wash themselves with fresh water as soon as possible after getting out; however, these chemical peculiarities are

56-57
*Jordanians appreciate the
many curative properties of
the Dead Sea.*

57 bottom left
*The Dead Sea is geologically
and chemically unique.*

57 bottom right
*The Dead Sea Spa Hotel is
a modern bathing complex
offering every comfort.*

58 top left
An eloquent view of Wadi al-Mujib.

58 centre left
The bare hills that surround the Dead Sea have a wild beauty.

58 bottom left
Bathers on the shores of the Dead Sea.

58 right
Sunset over the Dead Sea.

59
Another view of the lovely Wadi al-Mujib.

highly therapeutic and consequently a renowned resort is situated about 30 miles from Amman at Suwaymah where skin diseases and respiratory ailments are treated. Close by, near the village of Zarqa Main, the many thermal springs are used in a modern complex to treat rheumatism and dermatitis and there is also an extraordinary hot waterfall that gives off dense clouds of steam as it gushes down.

Besides the particular properties of its water, the Dead Sea is surrounded by an unusual landscape. Strange crystalline formations are to be found on its shores and the rocks that line the edge of the water are curiously coloured and shaped. Wadi al-Mujib, a tributary of the great salt lake, deserves particular mention: the deep canyon, which can only be reached from the village of Dibhan, is one of the most striking places in Jordan as the water, that in some places can be canoed, creates spectacular contrasts with the intense blue of the sky.

Mount Nebo
THE TOMB OF THE PATRIARCH

60 top
The apse of the Basilica built during the Byzantine era.

60 centre
A cross has been erected on the spot where the death of Moses is commemorated.

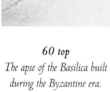

Six miles from Madaba and about 25 from Amman, Mount Nebo (Jebel Naba, 804 metres high) is supposed to have been the mountain that Moses was ordered to climb by the Lord in order to look over the Promised Land before dying. Indeed, on days when the sky is clear, the panorama is wonderful and it is possible to see right across the low Jordan valley to the Dead Sea and even as far as Jerusalem. Archaeological excavations by Franciscan monks since the

1930's on the western peak, Jebel al-Siyagha, have unearthed a three nave basilica which was built during the sixth century over the presumed tomb of the Patriarch that is now covered by a modern building. The apse is actually a primitive church in the shape of a trilobate cross that dates from the fourth century.

The Byzantine religious complex included a baptistery, the Chapel of the Virgin (the *Theotokos*) and a room known

as the diaconicon where the robes of
the priests were kept. A large monastery
used to stand next to the church. Inside
the basilica, the remains of decorated
capitals and some lovely floor mosaics
can be seen: the most outstanding (on
the right in the *diaconicón*) was created
in 531 showing hunting and grazing
scenes. It is divided into four sections
framed by an intertwining motif. Two
figures are shown in the lower section –

a white man and a black man – holding
a zebra, a dromedary and an ostrich by
their bridles.

The basilica also displays mosaics from
other buildings and churches in the area
which have been reset onto vertical panels
to distinguish them from its own. A
fragment taken from the church of St.
George showing two gazelles contains
Jordan's oldest known inscription in
archaic Arabic.

60 bottom
The interior of the Basilica
with its modern covering.

60-61
Excavation and
restoration works continue
uninterrupted in the area
of the Basilica.

ΕΜΝΗΘΗΤΙΤ ωΝΕΝΘΑΔΕΚΛΗΡΙΚωΝΤΕΚ ΜΟΝΑΧ
ΟΘΕΛΟΥΚΚΑΙΟΥ ΙΟΥΚω...Ι ΑΑΟΙΤ ωΝΚΠΑΝΤΟΟ

62-63
*The splendid floor mosaic in
the* diaconicón *showing
hunting and grazing scenes.*

62 bottom	**63 top**	**63 centre**	**63 bottom**
The diaconicón mosaic was discovered in 1976; note the base of the font on the left.	Many mosaics from other local buildings are kept in the Byzantine basilica.	The peacock was a symbol of immortality and often shown in early Christian art.	This mosaic contains the word "bisalameh" (in peace) written in archaic Arabic.

64-65
Hippolytus' Room with its
sixth-century mosaics.

64 bottom left
A detail of the mosaics in
Hippolytus' Room.

64 bottom right
On the right, Aphrodite sits
next to Adonis.

65 top

One of the Four Seasons in Hippolytus' Room.

Madaba
THE HOLY LAND REVEALED

The ancient city of Madaba lies 20 miles from Amman down the Kings' Highway. It is most famous for its splendid Byzantine floor mosaics that once decorated the many local Christian churches and public and private buildings. The best-known of these mosaics is the one kept in the Greek Orthodox basilica of St. George that was rebuilt in 1880. The mosaic is known as the "Map of Palestine" and shows the area bounded by the coast of Lebanon, the Nile delta, the Mediterranean and the desert. Although many parts have been destroyed during past renovations of the church, the remaining sections show 157 sites labelled in Greek with details of important buildings in the principal centres and mountains. The mosaic, which is made of roughly 2 million tiles, has been dated to the second half of the sixth century AD and is of immense importance for the study of the Holy Land during the Byzantine era. It shows the course of the river Jordan, the Dead Sea and the most important biblical sites such

65 centre

This detail of the "Map of Palestine" shows the city of Jericho in the centre (IEPIXΩ).

65 bottom

The mosaic in the church of St. George is one of the oldest known maps of the Holy Land.

as Jericho and Bethlehem. The largest city, Jerusalem, is immediately recognisable and scholars have identified no fewer than 38 streets and buildings, including the Church of the Holy Sepulchre.

Other buildings in Madaba that conserve important floor mosaics are the eighth-century church of the Virgin Mary, Hypolitus' Room (next door) in which a

mid-sixth-century mosaic depicts the Greek tragedy of the same name, the church of the Apostles with a mosaic of a female personification of the sea put down in 578, the Cathedral with its annexed chapels of the martyr Theodore (with mosaics bearing the date 562), and the Baptistery. Other fragments of mosaic are displayed in the Archaeological Museum.

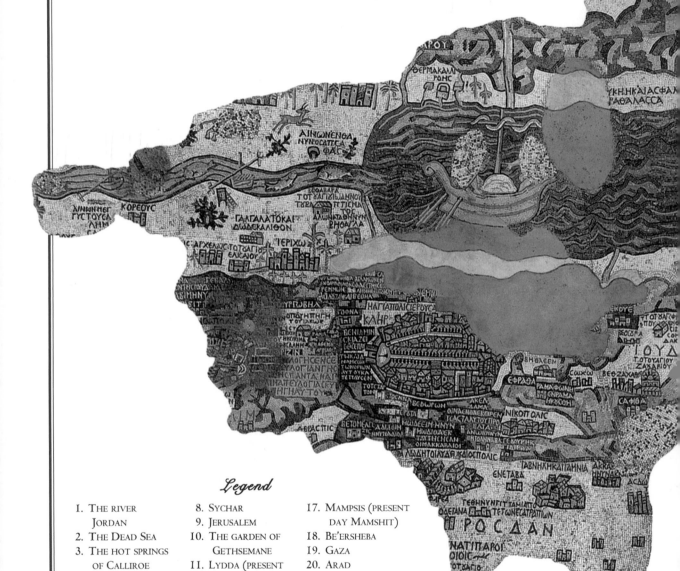

Legend

1. THE RIVER JORDAN	8. SYCHAR	17. MAMPSIS (PRESENT DAY MAMSHIT)
2. THE DEAD SEA	9. JERUSALEM	18. BE'ERSHEBA
3. THE HOT SPRINGS OF CALLIROE (PRESENT DAY ZARQA MAIN)	10. THE GARDEN OF GETHSEMANE	19. GAZA
	11. LYDDA (PRESENT DAY LOD)	20. ARAD
	12. NIKOPOLIS (BIBLICAL EMMAUS)	21. ELUSA
4. CHARACH MUBA (PRESENT DAY KARAK)	13. BETHLEHEM	22. PELUSIUM
	14. ELEUTHEROPOLIS (PRESENT DAY BEITH GUVRIN)	23. THE NILE DELTA
5. ARAVA DESERT	15. ASHDOD	
6. JERICHO	16. ASHKELON	
7. NEAPOLIS (PRESENT DAY NABLUS)		

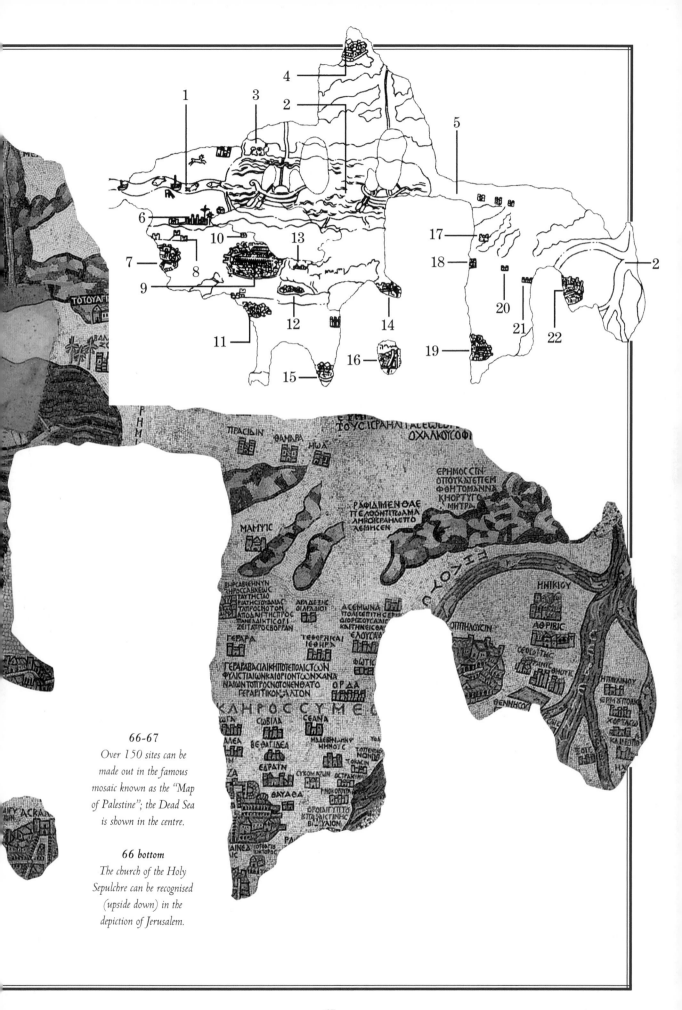

66-67

Over 150 sites can be made out in the famous mosaic known as the "Map of Palestine"; the Dead Sea is shown in the centre.

66 bottom

The church of the Holy Sepulchre can be recognised (upside down) in the depiction of Jerusalem.

68 top
*A view of the massive walls
of Karak castle*

Castles of the desert
THE CUSTODIANS OF AN EPIC PAST

The arresting remains of castles, fortresses, towers, thermal baths, caravanserais and palaces – known collectively as the "Castles of the Desert" – are found among the hills that stretch north and east of Amman and among the arid expanses in the southern regions towards Petra and Wadi Arabah. These constructions date from different periods of Jordanian history – from Roman and Umayyad domination and the Crusader era – but in some cases had no military or defensive purposes at all. Yet, as the origins of many of them have been lost from public consciousness, tradition has handed them down with this appealing label that suggests a bloody and epic past.

The most famous Jordanian castle is without question the one in Karak, a city about 80 miles from Amman on the Kings' Road. The modern town has been built on the site of Charach Muba, the ancient capital of the biblical kingdom of Moab. The city was in turn conquered by the Assyrians, the Nabataeans and the Romans before enjoying great prosperity under the Byzantines. Construction of the enormous stronghold that dominates the town was started in 1232 on the wishes of King Baldwin I in order to defend communications between Aqaba and Jerusalem from the Arab attacks. The last lord

68 centre
Karak castle is strategically positioned at 3,117 feet of altitude.

68 bottom
Note the original Crusader structures on the west face of Karak castle.

68-69
The south bastion of Karak castle was rebuilt by the Arabs in the thirteenth century.

69 bottom left
The echoes of a bloody past can still be heard among the ruins of Karak castle.

69 bottom right
A historical museum has been set up in some of the rooms of Karak castle.

70-71
The ruins of a black basalt palace at Umm al-Jamal.

70 bottom left
The remains of the castle of Qal'at al-Rabat near Ajlun.

70 bottom right
One of the rooms inside Qal'at al-Rabat castle.

71 top
The Praetorian Palace (370 AD) is one of the best conserved structures at Umm al-Jamal.

of Karak was the cruel Renauld of Chatillon who used to throw prisoners to their death from the battlements; once the castle had been taken by Sultan Saladin in 1189, it was abandoned until the end of the sixteenth century.

The ruins of Umm al-Jamal, a city founded by the Nabataeans and later conquered by the Romans, lie on the border with Syria to the north east of Amman. After becoming part of the Byzantine empire, it fell into the hands of the Umayyad caliphs during the seventh century and experienced a period of splendour but it was never rebuilt after being razed to the ground by an earthquake, and today seems a "dead city" of monumental ruins unusual for the peculiar dark colour of the basalt with which it was built.

72 top
A detail of the Umayyad frescoes at Qasr Amrah.

72 bottom
The interior of the throne room at Qasr Amrah.

The castle of Qal'at al-Rabat near Ajlun in the north of the country, about 45 miles from Amman, is one of the most exceptional examples of Islamic military architecture of the twelfth and thirteenth century. It seems that it was used as a base by Saladin during his victorious offensive against the Crusaders which culminated in 1187 with his capture of Jerusalem.

Built as a sumptuous hunting lodge by Umayyad Caliph Walid I (705-715) and not as a fort, Qasr Amrah, situated 21 miles east of Amman, is celebrated for its magnificent internal frescoes. Scenes of daily life and hunting, warriors, music, dancers and even naked young women bathing are depicted on the walls and vaults; this is exceptional for the Moslem world which forbids the reproduction of the human figure. In all probability, the caliph was a liberal man who appreciated art.

Not far from Amman, Qasr al-Mushatta is another Umayyad building designed as a fortified palace by Caliph Walid II. It too should have been decorated with bas-reliefs, plasterwork and mosaics but the construction was never completed. Today there only remain the imposing ruins of the throne room and a few adjoining rooms.

72-73 and 73 bottom right
The remains of Qasr Amrah comprise the three-nave throne room, the hammam (baths) next door and what is left of a well and tank.

73 bottom left
A zodiac is depicted in the frescoes on the dome of the hammam.

74-75

The hill where the remains of Macheonte (today known as Mukavir) lie; Macheonte is the fort where Salome danced for King Herod.

Qasr al-Hallabat was built by the Romans 19 miles east of Amman during the second century AD as a defensive fort but it was turned into a monastery during the Byzantine era and then became a palace for rest and pleasure under the Umayyad caliphs. Unfortunately it too has been reduced to ruins but gives some indication of its past splendour.

Seventy five miles further east in the green oasis of Azraq stands the fort (*qasr*) of the same name which was founded by the Romans between 286-305. It was later occupied during the Umayyad era and rebuilt in 1236.

To the south on a crossing point of ancient caravan routes, Qasr al-Karanah is the best conserved of the Castles of the Desert. Built on a four sided plan with a circular tower at each corner, it was probably constructed by an Umayyad caliph, perhaps in 711.

Finally, Ash Shawbak perches on a rise that overlooks the Kings' Road to the south of Karak. It was built in 1115 by Baldwin I and is known as *Mons Regalis*. It was captured by Saladin in 1189 and later occupied by the Mamelukes.

74 bottom left and 74 bottom right

Two view of Qasr al-Azraq, completely built from black basalt.

75 top and 75 centre

The magnificent fortified palace of Qasr al-Mushatta was never completed.

75 bottom

An elegant polylobate doorway at Qasr al-Hallabat.

76 top
*One of the vaulted
rooms at Qasr
al-Karanah.*

76 bottom
*The remains of a hammam
can be seen at as-Sarah near
Qasr al-Hallabat.*

76-77
*The massive Qasr
al-Karanah.*

77 bottom left
*The ruins of the Roman
temple at Ar-Rabbah built
in the third century AD.*

77 bottom right
*A view of the baths at
as-Sarah.*

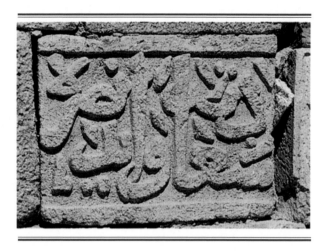

78 top
An Arab inscription in the castle of Ash Shawbak.

78 centre
An aerial view of the castle at Ash Shawbak.

78 bottom
The Crusader chapel in the castle at Ash Shawbak.

78-79
The fort at Ash Shawbak perched on the top of a hill along the Kings' Road.

79 bottom left
The remains of the Crusader church in the castle of Ash Shawbak.

79 bottom right
Some Crusader, Arab and Mameluke finds displayed in the castle of Ash Shawbak.

Petra
THE ROSE-RED CITY OF THE NABATAEANS

Legend

1 WADI MUSA
2 PETRA FORUM REST HOUSE
3 ENTRANCE GATE
4 BROOKE HOSPITAL
5 DJINN BLOCKS
6 OBELISK TOMB AND BAB AL SIQ TRICLINIUM
7 TRIUMPHAL ARCH
8 NABATAEAN TUNNEL
9 SIQ
10 KHASNEH

11 HIGH PLACE OF SACRIFICES
12 OBELISKS
13 LION MONUMENT
14 GARDEN TOMB
15 ROMAN SOLDIER TOMB AND TRICLINIUM
16 RENAISSANCE TOMB
17 BROKEN PEDIMENT TOMB
18 THEATRE

19 TOMB OF UNEISHU
20 ROYAL TOMBS
21 TOMB OF SEXTIUS FLORENTINUS
22 CARMINE FAÇADE
23 HOUSE OF DOROTHEUS
24 COLONNADE STREET
25 TEMPLE OF THE WINGED LIONS
26 COLUMN OF THE PHARAOH
27 QASR AL BINT

28 OLD MUSEUM
29 NEW MUSEUM
30 LION TRICLINIUM
31 ED DEIR
32 TOWN WALLS
33 TURKAMANYYA TOMB
34 ARMOUR TOMB
35 NICHE OF THE EAGLE
36 AQUEDUCT
37 CRUSADER CASTLE OF AL WU'EIRA

80 top
The huge tholos that crowns the Deir.

80 bottom
A view of the Deir from Jebel Harun.

81 bottom
Aeolian erosion at Petra has produced unusual shapes.

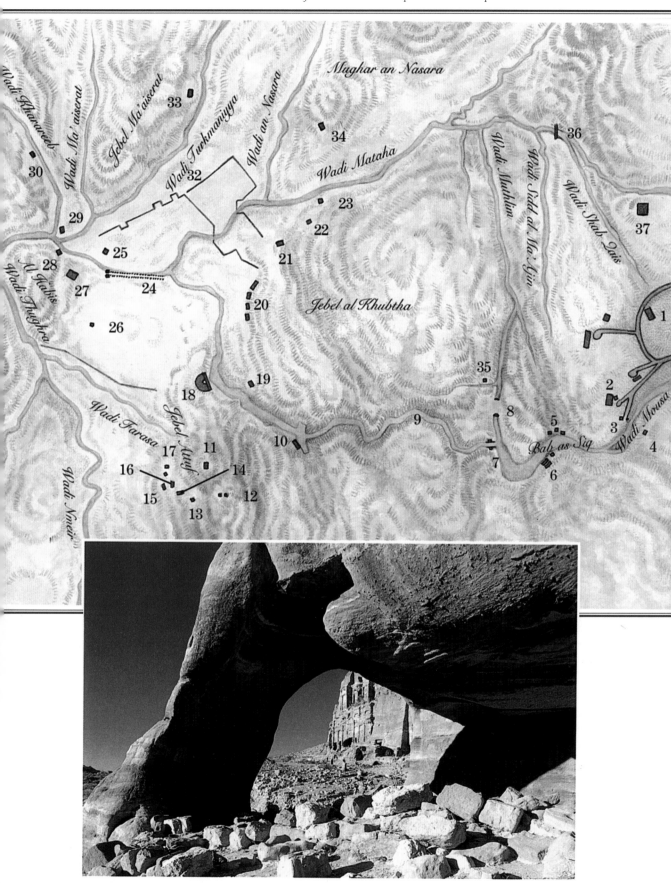

Wadi Khanareeb

Wadi Ma'aiserat

Jebel Ma'aiserat

Wadi Turkmaniyya

Wadi an Nasara

Mughar an Nasara

Wadi Mataha

Wadi Mudlim

Wadi Sidd al Ma'ajin

Wadi Shab Qais

Wadi Thughra

Al Habis

Jebel al Khubtha

Wadi Farasa

Jebel Attuf

Wadi Nmeir

Bab as Siq

Wadi Mousa

82-83
The Obelisk Tomb and,
below, the Bab al Siq

Triclinium (both first century
AD) stand almost opposite the
Djinn Blocks.

82 bottom left and 82 bottom right
The Djinn Blocks stand close to Wadi Musa along the Bab al Siq: these strange monolithic blocks were perhaps first-century BC tombs.

The ruins of Petra are one of the most extraordinary archaeological complexes from antiquity, both for the buildings cut out of the rock that make it so unusual and for the city's wonderful location between steep rock faces and deep gullies.

This unique place was known in the Bible as *Sela'*, "rock" in Hebrew; the Arabs called it Wadi Musa, "the valley of Moses" while the name Petra is the Greek translation of the Biblical name. Although the oldest known settlement at Petra dates back to the Iron Age, the importance of the city is derived from its occupation by the Nabataeans during the fourth century BC. The Nabataeans were nomads from the Arabian peninsula but once they became a settled people, they organised themselves into a solid monarchy with an economy based on trade. Starting in the third century BC, Petra was turned into a rock city in a

84 top left
The Siq is a spectacular chasm caused by an earthquake.

84 centre left
The inner room of the Khasneh with sides measuring 42 feet.

84 bottom left
The façade of the Khasneh (128'8" high) was dug out of a wall of the Siq.

84 right
One of the capitals that adorn the Khasneh.

85
The Khasneh has been dated to a period between the second half of the first century BC and the first half of the first century BC. It is thought it was the tomb of a king, perhaps Obodas II or Aretas IV.

valley where several gullies meet. Its choice as the Nabataean capital was motivated by reasons of safety as, being hidden among mountains and having few means of access that were easily guarded, it was an ideal refuge. The short and easy journey to the Red Sea allowed exchanges to take place with Arabia and Mesopotamia, while the track across the Negev to Gaza gave access to the Mediterranean and the ports of Syria. Continuous dealings with the important commercial routes and traders and the city's growing prosperity brought about its hellenisation, evident from the monuments cut out of the rock during the first century AD. Occupation of Petra by the Romans and its annexation to the province of Arabia – which took place in 106 AD under Trajan – slowed but did not halt development; however, with the rise of other caravan centres such as Gerasa and Palmyra, the importance of Petra began to diminish. For several centuries, the rock city continued prosperous and was designated as a bishopric, but after the Arab conquest of the region, it fell into total decline though it

86 top
*The stage of the Theatre,
destroyed by an
earthquake, dates from the
Roman era.*

86 bottom
*Many Assyrian-style
tombs line the Siq near the
Theatre.*

86-87
*The Theatre could hold
6000 spectators.*

87 bottom left
*The Tomb of Uneishu
stands almost opposite the
Theatre. It dates from
between 70 and 76 AD.*

87 bottom right
*Once past the Theatre, the
Siq widens into a plain
where the proper city stood.*

was briefly fortified against the Crusaders. At the end of the thirteenth century, it was completely abandoned and forgotten about in the West until 1812 when it was rediscovered by Johann Ludwig Burckhardt, the famous Swiss traveller and orientalist.

The unusual appearance of the capital of the Nabataeans had already made it the object of admiration and amazement 2000 years ago. The single easy access to the city was along the bed of Wadi Musa, the torrential river that crossed the residential area where hotels now stand. A short distance beyond the first rock buildings – the Djinn Blocks, the Obelisk Tomb and the Bab al Siq Triclinium below – the valley is transformed into a narrow ravine known as the Siq whose waters are deviated into a side gully. The gorge (along which Petra's main aqueduct also ran) is 585 feet deep and the two walls are no more than 12 feet apart in places. Where the chasm suddenly changes direction, Petra's most famous building appears, the Khasneh, a superb funerary temple carved from the delicate pink rock. The façade is 130 feet high and 81 feet wide. The lower floor has a gable portico with six Corinthian columns each 42 feet high. The upper floor is divided into three sections. In the centre there is a *tholos* (a

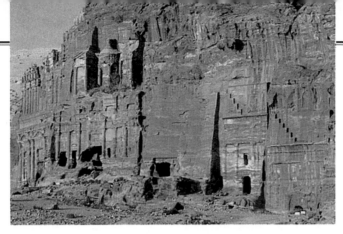

88 top
A view of the Royal Tombs with the Corinthian Tomb on the left.

88 bottom
This is the splendid tomb (129-130 AD) of the Roman envoy Sextius Florentinus.

88-89
The opening downstream of the Siq and the wall where the Royal Tombs were carved.

89 bottom left
The Tomb of the Urn which may hold the remains of king Aretas IV who died in 40 AD.

89 bottom right
The polychrome Silk Tomb.

90 top
A detail of the grandiose
Palace Tomb.

90 centre
The multi-coloured interior
of a rock building.

90 bottom
The hypogean room of the
Tomb of Uneishu.

small round temple) with a conical roof topped by an urn which is what has given the building its Arabic name, i.e. "Treasury". The Bedouin thought that the urn contained immense riches and shot at it several times with their rifles in the attempt to smash it open. The *tholos* is flanked by two half-gables in which reliefs of horsewomen appear in niches. Inside the building a hall leads into the main room in the shape of a large cube measuring 39 feet each side with smaller burial niches on three sides.

A little past the Khasneh, the Siq widens. On the left, the 6000-seater theatre is dug out of sheer rock, while opposite are located what are known as the Royal Tombs (the Tomb of the Urn, the multi-coloured Silk Tomb, the elegant Corinthian Tomb and the gigantic Palace Tomb) all of which have been dated to the first century AD.

The area that contained the residential area – now mostly destroyed by earthquakes – is in the shape of an amphitheatre enclosed by high steep walls in which the Nabataeans excavated a large number of tombs and rock dwellings. The wide valley, crossed by the Wadi Musa (usually dry) measures a little over a mile from east to west and half a mile from north to south.

The summits of the surrounding hills

93 centre
The Temple of the Winged Lions was built during the first half of the first century BC.

93 bottom
The Unfinished Tomb lies in the rock wall known as al Habis.

92-93
The Colonnade Street to the left and the Gate of Temenos, the holy esplanade.

92 bottom right
The temple known as Qasr al Bint is the only constructed building remaining in Petra.

92 bottom left
The Colonnade Street, the main road at Petra, dates from the Roman era.

93 top
The purpose of the hypogean Columbarium with niches remains a mystery.

94 bottom right
This effigy of Zeus is found
along the steps to the
Old Museum.

95 top right
This fragment of a capital
is evidence of Greek influence
on local art.

95 left
A lovely bas-relief
displayed in the old
Archaeological Museum.

95 bottom right
The Nabataeans incorporated
figurative modes from the Greek
and Roman worlds into their art.

were the sites of places of worship and the forts that defended the means of access to the city. The main entrance, entirely colonnaded, began near a *nymphaeum*; a little further on stand three markets set on sloping terraces with shops along the sides, the Great Temple, the Temple of the Winged Lions, the Gate of Temenos (the holy esplanade) and the temple known as Qasr al Bint, the only structure to have been built as opposed to excavated that has remained standing. The new Archaeological Museum stands close by from which a path leads off into a gorge before turning into a steep flight of steps. 1140 feet up, the path finally arrives at the Deir or Monastery. Dating from the first century AD, the Deir is unquestionably the most impressive building in the Nabataean capital. Cut entirely out of the rock, the façade of the funerary temple measures 160 feet wide by 127 high. The lower floor is lined by pillars and there are 8 semi-columns that frame two niches at the sides and a gable doorway

94-95
A bas-relief displayed in the
Old Museum.

94 bottom left
A room in the new
Archaeological Museum.

This male bust of the god Serapis adorns the entrance to the Old Museum.

This head of the god Hermes has been influenced by eastern art.

The interior of the old Archaeological Museum.

A panel depicting a sphinx.

This bust of Aphrodite adorns the Gate of Temenos.

in the centre. The entrance leads into a large square room with a niche in the back wall where the altar stands. The façade on the upper floor contains a central *tholos* and, to either side, two solid semi-gables and avant-corps. The various architectural details on the second floor are linked by a lovely Doric frieze. Seen from the hill in front of the Deir, the view takes in all of the valley in which Petra stands but the best place to see the Rose-Red City is without doubt the top of Jebel Attuf where an open air sanctuary, the "High place of sacrifices", can be reached by a steep path that begins near the Theatre. From here, Petra truly seems part of a dream world and not a splendid reality.

99 top
*Two of the three naves in the
church are decorated with mosaics.*

99 bottom
*The subjects of some
paintings show the Seasons.*

98-99
*The remains of a church
with splendid mosaic
flooring are also found at
Petra.*

98 bottom left
*The church mosaics date
from the sixth century AD.*

98 bottom right
*The subjects of the mosaics
are partly taken from
classical traditions.*

100 top
The Deir is the most impressive monument at Petra.

100 centre
The covering of the tholos *in the Deir is 38 feet high.*

100 bottom
Wadi Arabah lies near the Deir.

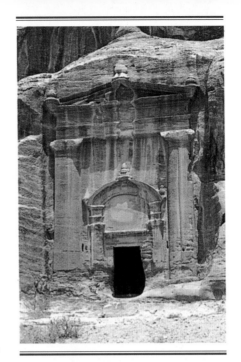

**102-103 and 102
bottom left**
*The Garden Tomb and its
interior.*

102 bottom right
*The Broken Pediment
Tomb.*

103 top
*The elegant Renaissance
Tomb.*

103 centre
*The Tomb of the Roman
Soldier: like the others on
this page, this is found in
Wadi Farasa,
along one of the two paths
that climb Jebel Attuf.*

103 bottom
*The triclinium in front
of the Tomb of the
Roman Soldier.*

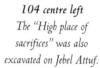

104 top left
The two obelisks on Jebel Attuf, symbols of the gods Dushara and Al Uzza.

104 bottom left
The entrance to the Painted House in the area of Al Barid.

104 centre left
The "High place of sacrifices" was also excavated on Jebel Attuf.

104 top right
A view of Al Barid, a rock settlement a few miles from Petra.

104 bottom right
This monument is found in the Siq at Al Barid.

105
A rock temple at the entrance to Al Barid.

106 top
*A panoramic view from the
top of Jebel Attuf.*

106 centre
*The peak of Jebel Harun
(4,580 feet).*

106 bottom
*Several hours walk from
Petra on the peak of Jebel
Harun, stands a small
Islamic sanctuary built on
the tomb of Aaron, the
brother of Moses.*

106 – 107
Arón es venerado por los
musulmanes como profeta
del monoteísmo.

107 abajo, a la izquierda
Otra vista parcial de la
tumba de Arón, cuya fecha
de fundación es desconocida.

107 abajo, a la derecha
El peculiar monumento
nabateo llamado de la
Serpiente, en el Wadi Thughra.

108-109
Today Wadi Rum is a
nature reserve.

108 bottom left
Pinnacles of sandstone
dominate Wadi Rum.

108 bottom right
Inscriptions from the Thamudic
era (sixth-third century BC).

Wadi Rum
LAWRENCE'S DESERT

109 top

A solitary spiny acacia, a tree typical of Wadi Rum.

109 bottom

A spectacular natural arch produced by aeolian erosion.

The wide valley of Wadi Rum is one of the most famous and best loved places in Jordan. It is a fabulous setting where one can experience the authentic poetry of the desert. The depression is formed by the confluence of ancient *wadi* — torrential river beds —surrounded by steep walls, pinnacles and outcrops in the warm reddish tones of the rock. The two largest peaks in the country — Jebel Rum (5,758 feet) and Jebel Umm Ishrin (a fraction lower) — can be seen in the distance. Of majestic proportions, Wadi Rum was a transit point for millennia between Arabia and Palestine. Impossible as it seems, several springs flow into Wadi Rum allowing patches of vegetation to grow and so the *wadi* became an obligatory stopping point for the caravans carrying spices and incense from the kingdom of Sheba (modern-day Yemen) to the ports of the Mediterranean. The Nabataeans, however, were not the first to discover the precious water resources of Wadi Rum, later to be exploited by the

110 top
The Bedouin from the Howeitat tribe who have always lived in Wadi Rum are now a settled people.

110 bottom
A panorama of the desert near Wadi Rum.

110-111
Nature has modelled the rocks at Wadi Rum into bizarre shapes.

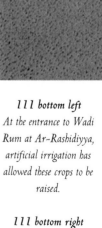

Romans: there are many rock carvings in the area which indicate human presence as far back as the Palaeolithic era. The present day heirs of the ancient inhabitants of Wadi Rum are the Bedouin who breed goats and dromedaries and whose young men form the backbone of the legendary Desert Police.

Famous for the rock formations eroded by the wind into surreal shapes, Wadi Rum is above all a symbol of national Jordanian independence. During World War I, the insurrectionists led by Lawrence of Arabia used this site as a camp before making the decisive attack on the fort of Aqaba which forced the Turks out of the country. It was in Wadi Rum that the English Major Lawrence, who fought side by side with the rebels of Emir Hussein I from 1916 to 1918, conceived his memoirs, *"The Seven Pillars of Wisdom"*, in which he described the wild beauty of this refuge, a beauty that still creates such an impression on the fortunate visitors to Wadi Rum.

111 bottom left
At the entrance to Wadi Rum at Ar-Rashidiyya, artificial irrigation has allowed these crops to be raised.

111 bottom right
A short distance away, however, the desert resumes.

112-113
The spectacular natural scenery
of Wadi Rum was made

famous in the 1962 film,
"Lawrence of Arabia", *by*
director David Lean.

114 top
*A guard in the legendary
Desert Police.*

114 centre
*Approximately 5000
Bedouins live in Wadi Rum.*

114 bottom
*The men of the Desert
Police wear the traditional
Jordanian white and red
kefiah on their uniform.*

114-115
*The Desert Police patrol the
most remote areas on
dromedaries.*

115 bottom left
*A Bedouin guides some
dromedaries over the bare
rocks of Wadi Rum.*

115 bottom right
*A Bedouin camp at Wadi
Rum; today there are fewer
than 45,000 real nomads
in Jordan.*

116-117
*Two Bedouins with their
faithful "ships of the desert".*

—Aqaba—

THE WINDOW ON THE RED SEA

Lying on the Aqaba gulf on the Red Sea, the city of Aqaba is Jordan's only port as well as being a thriving tourist resort. The city of roughly 35,000 inhabitants is placed right on the border with Israel and the westernmost districts are no more than a mile and a half from those of the cities of Eilat, its Israeli counterpart. Jordanian territory on the Red Sea only measures about 25 miles across which is occupied in part by a nature reserve, in part by the port and the rest is sandy beaches.

The city flourished during the times of King Solomon and then again during the first centuries of Islam under the name of *Ayla* but little remains of its long and glorious past except the fort. The massive square structure with four corner towers was built in the first half of the sixteenth century to protect pilgrims on their way to Mecca. Mostly rebuilt during the Ottoman

118 top
An aerial view of the centre of Aqaba.

118 bottom
A section of beach bordered by palm trees.

118-119
The houses in Aqaba are
dazzlingly white.

119 bottom left
A view of Aqaba with Eilat
on the horizon.

119 bottom right
Each hotel has its own
pleasure boats.

120-121
Relaxing on the beach.

120 bottom left
A view of the local Folklore Museum.

120 bottom right
A row of luxury hotels lines the seafront.

domination, the fort was attacked in August 1917 by rebel Bedouin tribesmen led by Lawrence of Arabia and Prince Feysal, son of Sheikh Hussein I. The defeat of the Turkish garrison marked the beginning of the path to independence and the birth of the modern kingdom of Jordan. There is a small but interesting archaeological museum next to the fort.

Aqaba is mostly known for its crystalline waters populated by flashing multicoloured fish, turtles and sea fans; it is a real paradise for sub-aqua enthusiasts. The city's tourist industry received a boost following the peace treaty signed in 1994 between the kingdom of Jordan and the state of Israel and today the white city on the cobalt sea is equipped with modern hotels, excellent restaurants and diving facilities to satisfy the most demanding of visitors.

121 top and 121 centre
The atmosphere in Aqaba is pleasantly relaxed.

121 bottom
Aqaba is one of the favourite holiday resorts of Jordanians because of its climate: mild in winter and kept cool by breezes in summer.

122 top
The coat of arms of the
Hashemite royal family is
displayed at the entrance to
the fort.

122 centre
Many mural inscriptions
record the fort's history.

122 bottom
The fort was founded by
Emir Khayir Bey al-Alai.

122-123
Each side of the recently
restored fort measures
about 54 yards
in length.

The entrance to the fort
where Lawrence of Arabia
and the Bedouin rebels
passed.

123 bottom right
Aqaba fort is one of the
symbols of Jordanian
national independence.

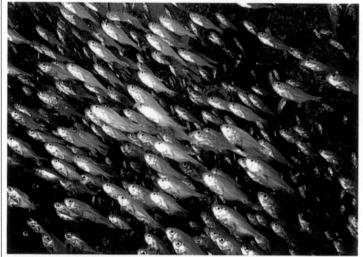

124 top
A grouper fish
(Cephalopholis miniata).

124 centre
A shoal of glass fish
(Pempheris vanicolensis).

124 bottom
A clown fish (Amphiprion
bicinctus).

124-125
A forked tail grouper
(Variola louti).

125 bottom left
Masked butterfly fish
(Chaetodon semilarvatus).

125 bottom right
A multicoloured branch of
alcyonaria.

126-127
The bare mountains
that surround Aqaba
change colour with the
time of day creating
scenes of incomparable
beauty.

Cover:
the superb facade of the
Khasnè at Petra.

All the photographs in the book are by Massimo Borchi and Giulio Veggi/ White Star Archive except for the following:

NASA: pages 8 and 9;

White Star Archive: pages 10, 11, 12, 13, 14, 15, 16, 17, 124 and 125;

Padre Michele Piccirillo: 66-67;

Antonio Attini/White Star archive: pages 116-117;

The map on pages 6-7 is by Cristina Franco.
The maps on pages 41, 67 and 80-81 are by Monica Falcone Bourbon.

INDEX OF PLACE-NAMES

Ain Ghazal: 11.
Ajlun (massif): 8.
Ajlun (city): 71, *70.*
Al Barid: *104.*
Amman: 8, 11, 12, 13, 14, 18, 20, 22, 25, 27, 39, 40, 48, 51, 58, 60, 65, 68, 71, 72, 75, *7, 18, 23, 29, 30, 34, 35.*
Aqaba (gulf): 8, 11, 12, 27, *8, 11.*
Aqaba (city): 12, 14, 17, 68, 110, 118, 121, *7, 10, 114, 121, 122, 124.*
Araq al-Amir: 39, *38.*
Ar-Rabbah: 76, *76.*
Ar-Rashidiyya: *110.*
Ash Shawbak: 12, *75, 78.*
Ayla: 118.
Azraq (city): 11.
Azraq (oasis): 9, 75.
Balqa: 14.
Charach Muba: see Karak.
Dead Sea: 8, 11, 52, 56, 58, 60, 66, *8, 54, 56, 57, 58, 67.*
Dibhan: 58.
El-Beidha: 11.
Fahl: 48.
Gadara: 12, 51.
Gerasa: see Jerash.
Ghor: 8.
Great Rift Valley: 8.
Habis, al: *93.*
Hammam as-Sarah: *76.*
Hor (Mount): *10.*
Irbid: 14, 51, *35.*
Jebel ar-Rimah: 8.
Jebel al-Asfar: 8.
Jebel Ashrafiyah: 22.
Jebel Attuf: 97, *103, 104, 106.*
Jebel Harun: 12, *11, 12, 81, 106.*
Jebel al-Jawfah: *27.*
Jebel Mubrak: 8.
Jebel Naba: see Nebo (Mount).
Jebel al-Qalah: 22.
Jebel Rum: 8, 109.
Jebel al-Siyagha: 60.
Jebel at-Taj: 22.
Jebel Umm Ishrin: 109.
Jerash: 12, 13, 17, 40, 42, 45, 84, *5, 46, 49.*

Jordan: 8, 9, 11, 12, 14, 48, 52, 54, 56, 60, 66, *8, 53, 54, 55.*
Karak: 12, 13, 14, 36, 68, 75, *33, 68, 69.*
Ma'an: 14.
Macheronte: see Mukavir.
Madaba: 36, 60, 65, 66, *36.*
Mafraq: 14.
Mount Nebo: 60, *5.*
Mukavir: 75.
Pella: 12, *48, 49.*
Petra: 11, 12, 13, 14, 17, 27, 68, 83, 84, 86, 97, *4, 10, 12, 13, 14, 16, 31, 81, 91, 93, 95, 99, 100, 104, 106.*
Philadelphia: 27.
Qal'at al-Rabat: 72, *70, 71.*
Qasr al-Azraq: 75, *75.*
Qasr al-Hallabat: 75, *75, 76.*
Qasr al-Karanah: 75, *76.*
Qasr al-Mushatta: 72, *75.*
Qasr Amrah: 72, *72, 73.*
Rabbath Ammon: 11, 27.
Red Sea: 84, 118.
Sela': 83.
Siq: 86, 90, *16, 84, 86, 88, 104.*
Suwaymah: 58.
Tabaqat al-Fahl: 48.
Tafilah: 14, 36.
Umm al-Jamal: 71, *70, 71.*
Umm Qays: 51.
Wadi Arabah: 8, 68, *8, 12, 100.*
Wadi Farasa: *103.*
Wadi Jirm al Moz: 48.
Wadi al-Mujib: 58, *58.*
Wadi Musa: 83, 86, 90, *83.*
Wadi Rum: 36, 109, 110, *4, 7, 108, 109, 110, 111, 114, 128.*
Wadi Sabra: *10, 12.*
Wadi as-Sir: *38.*
Wadi Thughra: *107.*
Wadi Zarqa: *54, 55.*
Zarqa: 14.
Zarqa Main: 58.

Standard format numbers refer to the text, numbers in italics refer to the photograph captions.